A PLACE TO BLOOM

A PLACE TO BLOOM

ETON LANGFORD

Irving Poetry Press

2000

ISBN-10: 0692374876

ISBN-13: 978-0692374870

CONTENTS

DEDICATION

To whom the simple joys of rhyme
  Are strongly indicated,
These scribbles of my tranquil time
  Are humbly dedicated.

Eton Langford

THEATRE

a tribute to Christopher Marlowe

AN ACTOR'S grind can be intense:
His stage craft must delight each sense;
In joy or grief, he should ring true
And pour his tumult out anew.

It is no light or facile task
To wear in life a different mask
And take the courage to express
Great passions painful to confess.

Whoever wishes to take aim
At immortality must claim
The highest prize on earth to find:
Remembrance in the public's mind.

Theatre merits for high esteem,
For acting is a graceful dream
Which grows on stage and takes to heart
The essence of dramatic art.

REDWOODS

a tribute to William Wordsworth

BEYOND the grove of giant ferns,
The mossy path descends and turns
Toward the glade of redwood trees,
Where mountains meet the dewy breeze.

Enveloped by the heavy fog,
The birds glide free across the bog
And burst into delightful calls
Over the chime of waterfalls.

In this abode, the giants loom
With lilies at their roots in bloom.
Their will transcends both space and time:
Their thoughts cannot be set to rhyme.

When I return the gift of birth
And I am doomed to leave this earth,
My peaceful soul shall stay to be
Embodied in this harmony.

THE ASTRONOMER

a tribute to George Gordon Byron

AWAY from the city, concealed from the world
On top of the mountain asleep in the cold,
A humble astronomer stares at a star.
How lonesome our planet must seem from afar!

He ponders the spaces of wearisome void,
Lost empires, celestial, unknown or destroyed,
Continuous mingling of matter and light.
Such frightening pageant for man's feeble sight!

The whirl of the spheres, the clash of the orbs,
Our universe dictates and calmly absorbs
With æons to spare and inscrutable plan.
How weak and unfit is the power of man!

ON THE MOUNTAINSIDE

a tribute to the high Romantics

UPON the mountainside, there flowed a stream of gold.
His subtle whisper carried him along the gorge,
Where firs and pines and maples, in the crevice, forge
Their nest of eagles sheltered by the rocky mould.

I hurried down to watch and chase his rapid pace,
Unbound though evanescent as the dew of dawn.
A thoughtful murmur was his voice, shy and withdrawn,
Entranced by lazy fog and donned in sprightly grace.

"Where do you wend your way? How were you born?" I said.
"I can't recall," he whispered, "sadly, I forgot,
But I don't need to know!" I added: "But why not?
Quite surely, you must reckon where and how to tread."

"Oh, no, dear lad, I am no kin of mortal man!
I brave these mighty rocks and ripple day and night;
I need no whither, whence: indeed, I am the might
Which guides the course of Nature and her clever plan!"

"I'll bear all living things within my wide embrace,
  And quench their weary thirst until the end of time.
  I see them grow and live and love and turn to slime;
  I know men well: they surely vanish without trace!"

"You stand and watch me as I slide and rush along,
  And think that I am only transient while you're firm.
  But no! Whereas I glide on royally, you squirm
  And Death, one day, will surely come to prove you wrong!"

"The likes of you need annals, chronicles and books
  To tell you plainly whither, why and how and whence.
  But I need neither purpose, strategy nor sense,
  For I encompass forest, mountain, field and brooks."

"Go forth, now! Take your fleeting chance to breathe and love
  Before your time is severed by the axe of fate!
  Oh, do not linger! Men are always slow and late,
  Despite their boundless thirst for endless life above!"

THE COOL OCEAN BREEZE

THE COOL ocean breeze,
On nights warm as these,
Is blowing with ease
While we sail the seas.

The moon and the tide
Have nothing to hide,
And bravely we ride
With stars as our guide.

We cruise over green
Dominions marine,
Indulging unseen,
Unheard and serene.

On ripples of bliss,
We roll as we kiss.
Oh, friend, never miss
A journey like this!

KNOWLEDGE CHAIN

a tribute to John Keats

THE DUSTY book in front of me
Was written centuries ago
And, in its youth, it was a tree
Whose story's not for man to know.

This tome was carried in the hands
Of lettered men who proudly owned
And turned its pages, soft as sand,
To read of exploits hardly known.

They learned of dynasties and kings
Whose memory would now be gone
If only these leaves did not sing
Of how man's straws were set and drawn.

The scholars died. The book survived,
Although its knowledge chain was broken
When no one bothered to revive
Its language, now so rarely spoken.

THE DAYS OF YOUTH

a tribute to William Wordsworth

THE DAYS of youth have hurried past,
And even friendships hardly last.
Before too long, I'll drift away
And blend with every passing day.

A year, a decade, even more
Will overthrow what stood before
And, unawares, I'll come to find
My dearest things all far behind.

I've walked through life and seen anew
That constancies are far and few,
That all beloved ones must go,
And that all life must ebb and flow.

Until the very end I'll see
Young love aspiring to be free,
And know that even its own fate
Will turn around before too late.

I will admire its gentle shine
And then recall when I had mine,
When courage blended with the sky,
On whose clear hope I could rely.

And then I shall walk by and smile
Though beauty only lasts awhile:
What draws and anchors me to stay
Are longing days which fly away.

I PEER INTO YOUR EYES

a tribute to William Shakespeare

I PEER into your eyes and long to dream
Of tranquil seas reigned over by the moon,
Of frisky mornings and their stunning gleam,
Or the proud skylark and its flowing tune.
I touch your downy skin and try to feel
The soft caress of dew on tender moss,
Whose mild embrace can comfort, soothe and heal
The aching grip of bitter grief and loss.
I taste your tender lips and I forget
That both our youth and beauty fly away,
But then remember that I'm in your debt
In ways which I can never hope to pay.
    I think of you and then I understand
    How blessed I was to kiss you on the sand.

RIDDLE

a parody of Percy Bysshe Shelley

HOW DO men choose their course on earth?
Some live for power, riches, fame,
Or may disdain both death and birth,
Our human fate alone to blame.

In many hearts there's but the thirst
For pleasure, wine, a rowdy night,
While others put their duty first
If kindness is their guiding light.

Not many have been keen to delve
Within man's fickle soul to find
The answer to this riddle, shelved
In dark recesses of the mind.

Despite their science, skill or sight,
This mystery of greatest worth
Evades so many in their plight:
How do men choose their course on earth?

EPITAPH FOR A DREAMER

a satirical tribute to George Gordon Byron

DON'T wait for me! I'm flying breathlessly to find
The lonely days I spent in search of summer skies
Or lying crushed by fate and hopelessly resigned
To dire eternity upon the Bridge of Sighs.

Don't be distressed! I longed to vanish long ago,
Upon a gale of wind across a sea of time.
I thought that frank and dauntless youth could overthrow
The faded world of men and its inept design.

Don't linger here! Though I am roaming far away,
I am forever close and walk with you through life.
Think not too much of me, enjoy the passing day,
But raise a glass of wine to me when joy is rife.

WATER LILIES

a tribute to Richard Wilbur

I SAW white lilies floating on the lake
And thought of reeds bent forth over the marsh.
It is much easier, indeed, to take
The form of water lilies, and less harsh.

THE FELLED OAK

a tribute to William Cowper

THE OLD oak felled by man is no different from me,
Whose own dreams were shot down, carried off to the sea.
By the river, this tree had enduringly stood
'Til the villager maimed it for need of its wood.

Time anon, in its shade I would blissfully lie—
Now this solace has died with a thud and a sigh.
Once much loved by the birds and caressed by the sun,
It's now nothing to no one; its glory is gone.

In my youth, though I rested or played in its shade,
I cared not that its trunk could be hewn by the blade.
Now I sit on its stump and reflect on how brief
Was the leisure afforded to me before grief.

Though cut down by the axe and mistreated by fate,
The green shoots of new life will grow out before late;
And though time is unkind and man's caprice is blind,
Stronger twigs will branch out, as will hope in my mind.

In due course, a much taller, more beautiful tree
Will grow strong as the faith which now surges in me
And, before I am gone, I will harbor anew
The brave dream and old joy which are now out of view.

Come one day, by the river, young children will play
And will rest by an oak tree much taller than they,
But instead of repeating my errors of old,
What I write now they'll read, though by then I'll be cold.

They will learn of a man who lived there long before
And whom nature had roofed in his prime by the shore:
A young man full of dreams, staring up at the sky,
Much at peace and content by the oak where he'd lie.

The short course of our lives must run out before long,
But our memory lingers in rhyme and in song;
If the tree and the man both forgotten must be,
May posterity cherish these verses from me.

TERROR

HOW QUICK and cold must Terror be!
For long it slithers by, unfelt,
Until its victim cannot see
The blow of horror being dealt.

It waits in darkness long indeed
Allowing victims false aplomb,
Then blazes out with strength and speed
As bold and baneful as a bomb.

Relentless courage must have he
Who hunts this serpent in the night
Until, at last, his hand is free
Its head to sever with a scythe.

TWO SWALLOWS

a tribute to Robert Frost

I WANT a day of full repose
With only nature within sight,
For only then I truly might
Attain the peace which it bestows.

A while ago, two swallows came
To raise their younglings in a nest
Below my roof and I felt blessed,
But then they vanished all the same.

The chirping birds were scared away;
Their glade and merry woods are gone.
As for warm shelter, there is none
And, without birds, my life is gray.

I cannot blame their choice or rage
Against the deeds of my own kin;
Although man's craft and will can win,
A birdless world is but a cage.

THE CAPTIVE ANGEL

THE SNOW and coarse wind both plunge down over oceans
Unbound and unmeasured by obstinate sailors
Who drift while confronting relentless emotions
Like obdurate petrels and stoical whalers.

Imprisoned ashore on a cliff is a mourner
Whose wings have been severed by devious captors;
He peers through the mist as he hides in his corner:
How blithe is life's book, but how sad is his chapter!

Condemned to uncover eternity's cryptic
And coveted secrets, he ponders the vastness
Of solitude cloaking a recondite, mystic
Philosophy hidden with infinite deftness.

The high-soaring tower which serves as his prison
Stands firm by the mountains' impassable summits;
Escape though he might, how unfit is this season
Of menacing gales where the precipice plummets!

Beset by despair is this desolate being
Who once wished to flee his old life's empty guises;
How downcast he'd be to find out, upon fleeing,
That loneness and death are his only surprises!

THE PROUD AURORA

a parody of the high Romantics

LET LARKING bliss on zephyr wings descend
And meadows fill with gleeful mirth and song;
The proud aurora's sparkle then amend
With daisies spread in their ambrosial throng.
   The cheerful gods pour nectar into grails,
   And the Elysian Fields unveil new trails.

Not made by inner storms in wet lament
Nor wrung in waning light at lonely hours,
But dressed in asters and with lilac blent,
Alluring hungry bees to laden flowers:
   In such attire was passion brightly born,
   Swathed full in beams of love and never lorn.

The fragrant bed where bashful muses lie
To lose the world, forget and softly doze
Away for hours is yet the same place I
Plucked off your kiss as though from a red rose.
   I judged the bow of Cupid too benign
   Before I won your heart and you had mine.

BEYOND IMPOSING GATES

BEYOND IMPOSING gates there lies the place
Where charming children of the leisure class
Live out their carefree days at tranquil pace
And play patrician games on greener grass.

Across the street stands shyly a small boy
In beggarly attire all wet by rain:
He watches bound by grief and craves the joy
Which he is never destined to attain.

The view before him puzzles and defies
His dream of justice on this cheerless day.
He shakes his head, draws closer still and sighs,
But then he bites his lip and walks away.

SEASCAPE

ON WINGS of whisper seagulls rise
Like an unhurried, gracious fleet
Which sails upon a sea of sighs
And takes my dreams away with it.

The clouds and waves anoint the sky
With drops of myrrh and hues of blue
While colors blend and tower high
And masts glide freely out of view.

How soft and languid is the roll
Of vessels tethered to the pier!
I wonder if they hear the call
Of friends afar and fellows near.

They roll with jealousy and grief
While many others, far away,
Might float over a glowing reef
Or laze upon a peaceful bay.

But here, where seagulls roam above,
The sad and silent fellows weep
For fear their unrequited love
May die forgotten in the deep.

THE DEMIURGE

a parody of Percy Bysshe Shelley

PERPLEXED BY riddles and betrayed by time,
The lonely spirit travels far adrift
On the horizon's dim and distant line,
In search of other souls whose flight is swift.

From the eternal temple of the gods
Come roiling forth three dark and ruthless birds,
Which carry in their beaks three magic rods
Upon whose sight the dread of men is stirred.

The golden rods are dread, despair and death,
Which haunt all men throughout their mortal lives,
And whose dark curse is borne with every breath
By these three harpies rising from their hives.

Descending from the heavens they converge
While circling round and round the mountain top
Where, in the dwindling light, the senses merge
And even time itself comes to a stop.

The vast expanses of the earth divide
And, with loud thunder, lava gushes out
While mountains and the seas are torn aside,
Allowing clouds of sulphur smoke to spout.

The birds of prey unchain the lightning storm
Upon the mighty mountain's snowy side
While in the depths of Hades there takes form
A demiurge of human shape and stride.

Emboldened by his grip on death and fear,
He rises tall, walks forth and calls to fight
The ghastly legions of the deep, who cheer
As mankind contemplates the growing night.

Olympus watches from above, unseen,
But worries not, for humans are no match
And Jove's revenge against all men has been
A treasured scheme which, finally, can hatch.

The helpless crowd, defeated, is dispersed
While darkness and despair engulf the scene
And servants of sly Jove become well versed
In hunting men to whom fair Hope is queen.

The world is turned into an endless maze
Where men are lost and wander all alone
While braving hunger, thirst and heavy haze
In search of hidden tunnels leading home.

They search in vain for what cannot be found,
Encouraged by false hope and blinding thought.
They rush away, bewildered and unbound
Along dim paths where rummage comes to naught.

Such was the day when man became a slave
To petty strife, to agony and death,
The day Olympus sentenced to the grave
All those on earth who labor and draw breath.

A CHIRPY BIRD

A CHIRPY bird with colored wings
    Lends solace everyday
To the great sage whose wisdom brings
    Advice to those astray.

The children taught by him are now
    The mighty of the land,
Yet when they see him pass they bow
    And humbly shake his hand.

He has no wealth which eyes can see,
    But he is glad and proud
That his disciples came to be
    Admired and praised aloud.

He could have spent his life in quest
    For nothing else but gold,
Yet, poor indeed, he feels so blessed
    His soul not to have sold.

THE ALCHEMY OF LOVE

WITH EVERY taste of wine and sweet perfume,
The florid touch of night grows ever wilder
And wraps the heart in evanescent bloom,
Which gives the mind new fantasies to ponder.

The crisp moscato rushes through the veins,
Unfurling blithe delights of youthful glories.
It is undue and fruitless to explain
The alchemy of love in sober stories.

THE RETURN OF THE SOLDIER

a parody of Henry Wadsworth Longfellow

VESTIGES, RUINS unchanged by the season,
Castles on mountains and fortresses linger.
Bleak is the night for the traveling stranger
Dragging his feet, a gold ring on his finger,
Battling the rain and consumed by his reason.

Years have elapsed since his mournful departure;
Family, friendships were left at the manor.
Bloody and restless was life under Ares,
Toiling and fighting the terrible banner
Held by a king with the skills of the archer.

Winds and the tempest subside into drizzle;
Sages and Druids convene by the fire,
Ponder the future and wait for the victor,
Weighing the sense of the gods' cruel desire,
Waiting for chatter and clamor to fizzle.

Gates open wide and the villagers gather,
Welcoming home the unfortunate fighter.
Children come forth with his brothers, all crying;
Gentler his fate should have been, and much lighter.
Cruel are the gods and implacable, rather!

THE WAILING BIRD

a parody of John Keats

BEHOLD THE wretched bird of joy and youth
Whose song was stolen by the winter night!
It wails with an undying thirst for truth
And barren valleys drape its lonely flight.

Soar high as liberty's unflinching friend!
Who else on earth can turn man's heart to joy
And his gray passions with true colors blend?
Return to sing of how life's bitter ploy

Has chained him down, and cleverly undone
His brightest dreams, the fabric etched in gold
Which you—and you alone—have nimbly spun!
Return to sing of how his dreams were sold!

Upon the worldly temple's steps I sit
And think of your light trills, all gone for long.
Unflaggingly I wait, a mourner's candle lit,
To hear your graceful voice and blissful song.

FLORA'S KISS

a satirical tribute to Alexander Pope

IN RIVER valleys and on golden hills,
Where spring's mild fragrance every taste fulfills,
The mind is set at peace by Flora's kiss:
Away from toil and grime, there's nothing one could miss.

The golden lyre's majestic, light accords
Exalt the song which nature's voice affords
And carry off to meadows near and far
The wondrous sound of Juno's soft guitar.

It's a delight to live a quiet dream
In a small house, in woods whose pathways teem
With birds and thrills, with days relieved of care:
A life of peace, of friendship everywhere.

THE FORGOTTEN TEACHER

a tribute to Oliver Goldsmith

THE CITY'S dark and silent streets
Are wet and cold in late November.
The trees stand still; a fireplace heats
A house which few care to remember.

In this forgotten, lonely place,
The heavy tomes entomb the teacher
While, in the dwindling light, his face
Betrays a soul of noble features.

In his cocoon, he has amassed
Much wisdom drawn from lengthy sorrow
While, unrelieved, his worries last
Far past the grim and hopeless morrow.

The world around him moves untouched
By knowledge, art or erudition,
For those who breathe don't care for much
Outside obtuse, absurd tradition.

He is a candle to the world
Whose light is seen by ever fewer:
His learning shrivels in the cold
Before the eyes of heedless viewers.

A THOUSAND WINTERS

a satire on erotic poetry

HOW GENTLY, next to me, you sleep,
How snug's our cradle, and how deep!
A thousand winters could well pass
And I would never miss May's grass.

Far off, outside, the snowy storm
Knows nothing of how smooth and warm
Is our embrace, and how complete
Our hearts become with every beat.

I muse so fondly on how true
Are my delight and love for you
And, as I see the sun's first beam,
I sink into a naughty dream.

SOME TRUTHS

a parody of Emily Dickinson

SOME TRUTHS may not be said out loud:
By thought alone it may be formed.
To make it known is not allowed
Because the plebe would be informed.

Some facts are noxious to the mob
And treated as deceptive schemes.
Woe to the man who tries to rob
The human race of hopeless dreams!

FIVE CURSES

a parody of George Gordon Byron

FOUL INFAMY! You sentenced to decay
The noble home anointed by young blood!
Its crumbling walls stand proof that you must pay
And that despair will drag you through the mud.

Deep misery! How glum and fateful it must be
   To see the errors of green youth at last,
   To taste of bitterness and sense the vast
And scorching desert of a conscience never free!

Grim idleness! The silver gleam of dawn
Is but a cloud of gloom upon your realm.
Unmoved by faith or hope, you whine and yawn
And wither in remorse when at the helm.

Blue melancholy! Dreadful is your heavy weight
   When lifeless winter plagues the sullen heart:
   Both hope and cherished dreams are torn apart
If cold remorse must sing its song and die too late!

Crass ignorance! How many times you've crashed
The ship of toil upon the shore of doom!
The boat defying soaring cliffs was smashed
The day you dug the mariners their tomb.

THE GOD OF GREED

a parody of Percy Bysshe Shelley

THE GOD of greed, of power and of haste
Has wrought in silence all the joy of love
From hearts of men and, in his anger, placed
His shield of gold upon the throne above.

Far down below, among the crowd dispersed
By petty brawls, debate and brutal screams,
His slaves sweat out with every breath immersed
In search of treasures and of silver streams.

The clever lord smirks slyly on his seat,
Amused that his devices are in swing
To daze the race of men. Let them repeat
The wrongs which, when committed, make him king!

Despite his craft, the master does not know
That somewhere far, well hidden from his stare,
A greater force, well known to be his foe,
Is stronger still, all-wise and truly fair.

This power trumps the lies and masquerade
Which avarice and fraud have set in place.
This ray of light, which does not fear the blade,
Is earnest Love, immune from all disgrace.

In her angelic shrine, she is unmoved
By selfish men, and boastful malice shown
To those who prize their honesty, who proved
That honest life is often life alone.

Unseen and quiet, she descends to aid
The weary and aggrieved who lose their way,
Who stumble blindly and whose powers fade
As they traverse the world in disarray.

The haughty master sees but worries not,
His aimless servants droning on bewitched,
But in the purest heart there lies a plot
Which, every minute, is by Love enriched.

With time and faithful patience, devotees
Of truth or fate and unrelenting grace
See, deep within, a vision which foresees
Relief from grief and justice for their case.

And thus, although the selfish men at large
Live out their days in lassitude or pride,
A few remain in the majestic barge
Of those who prove that kindness has not died.

Such is the world: a place of right and wrong,
Where those in power laugh—though they are blind—
And those who seek the truth are bold and strong,
Though very oft to silent pain confined.

Oh, reader, if you've loved, despaired and grieved,
Allow these humble words to urge and plead:
Though you were slighted, or indeed deceived,
May you forgive and be forever freed!

PEACE IN SOLITUDE

a tribute to William Shakespeare

WERE PEACE in solitude the wish of man,
The light of dawn could scorch it with its heat.
Were his great mind a large expanse of sand,
The dark blue sea could hide it in the deep.
Our hasty sun, undaunted, goes to sleep
And leaves behind a world beset by fools,
Whose great delight is learning how to keep
The honest man ignored and bound by rules.
Betrayed, the humble plod within the night
But feel no anger, grief, regret or fear:
The deep abyss itself can spread its light
When its rare crystals sparkle true and clear.
   May purest hearts rejoice a calmer sea,
   Avoid the world's abuse and wander free.

A SOLDIER'S MOTHER

WITH WRINKLED cheeks, with tearful eyes,
The frail old woman stares in space.
Distress and anguish fill her face;
Aggrieved and heavy are her sighs.

Her only son has died in fight
And her dear husband is long dead.
She feels no urge to look ahead;
There is no solace to her plight.

The feeble eyes behold the cane:
Such unfair dice were rolled and tossed!
A sea of tears she has now crossed
Yet many more, alas, remain.

Though she draws breath, she lives no more
And wonders hopelessly why those
Who rule the country ever chose
To stab her heart for want of war.

NATURE'S KEEP

a tribute to William Wordsworth

THE forest rich in hemlock, pine and oak
Lets rise aloft the loud voice of a stork;
This suddenly disturbs from their deep sleep
Small creatures hiding within nature's keep.

A ladybug is dancing on a stem
Like ruby strung on Aura's diadem.
Fair butterflies and playful skylarks fly
And bask in heat the rays of light supply.

In such a paradise of vivid green,
We are so transitory to be seen!
We are a breath of wind across the grass,
Whose vast dominion man cannot surpass.

May we then pause, stand still and not disturb
The precious gift of life, indeed superb.
May all embrace the message on this page,
So that the woods may thrive in every age.

RETURN, MY LOVE!

a tribute to George Gordon Byron

RETURN, MY love! Let's flee the gates to leave this scornful town,
And roam outside in deepest woods where Nature wears her crown!
Beside the river stands unmoved, as many years ago,
The ruined castle's narrow paths which you and I both know.

In there, where time has no abode, long centuries will pass
And seasons' splendors will unfurl their glint by the crevasse.
On summer nights, the glowing stars will watch us from above,
While nightingales and mockingbirds sing serenades to Love.

To the old turret we shall climb and watch the other shore,
Forget the world, unload our cares and never crave for more.
Our cradle on the mountainside all others will deter
Whereas, to us, its walls much peace and shelter shall confer.

Among those peaks the Sun is king and empress is the Moon,
And many times again they'll rise and never set too soon.
Over the mountains and the plains dominion we shall take
From crest to crest, across the vale, and further to the lake.

We'll never know the outer world, its burden and its need,
But rather seep from nectar cups which all our longings feed.
Behold, the summer wind has swept its hand across the glade
And, as its warmth enthralls the heart, our bliss shall never fade.

Not long ago I sought the place where we would often meet,
And found our mem'ry-laden bench by fairies softly lit.
The night was young, the air was warm and carried a fair scent,
While all the weeping willows were above the water bent.

I heard the crickets play in tune, unhurt by any care,
And, all around, the fireflies danced in this auspicious lair.
Descending on the marble steps I hurried down to watch
The moon reflected by the stream where fireflies we would catch.

The same white boat which, long ago, we used to go across
Was still beyond the reach of ferns enveloped by the moss.
I stepped inside and probed the depth in silence with an oar
And listened to the merry birds as many times before.

I paddled out into the flow of ripples wide and thin,
And felt the languid breeze of youth slide smooth across my skin.
The geese were tending to their young along the water's course
While, undisturbed, I came to feel the river's magic force.

The little lights upon the hill called out for me to come:
I sought a reason to return and, sadly, I found none.
All that I wished was, once again, that you'd return to me
And then together leave this world to roam forever free.

SAVIOR OF THE AGE

a tribute to Alexander Pope

ONE WORD upon another, on each page,
Goes prattling on the gossip of the age.
On very rare occasions does one see
Those worthy words which languish to be free.

At every corner, glimpses one can get
Of tiresome puppets of the art who fret:
All their delusions, dreams may never be
Much more than vile and vapid vanity.

From time to time, some poser on the stage
Pretends to be the savior of the age.
He shocks, amuses or evokes disdain
In those who must appraise his claim to fame.

Thus limping, mankind stumbles day by day
Along the path of ignorant display,
And few remain who wait and hope to see
The noble men who'd come to set them free.

THE THINKER

ON COLD and lonely nights,
When time holds no delights,
The thinker cannot sleep,
Though silence lingers deep.

The soft wind and the moon
Both glide away and soon
He's haunted by the might
Of man's eternal fight.

Dim light rays beam on down
As diamonds on a crown,
And yet he cannot see
How hope might set him free.

Much easier instead
Is following the thread
Of man's unstable will
Life's purpose to fulfill:

To wrestle in the storm,
Rejoice for being born,
To rise above the world,
Subdue his lust for gold,

To keep his banner tall,
Rise stronger from each fall,
And in the depths to find
The essence of his mind:

Strength, power, love and peace
When hope and love decrease,
When there's no rest or sleep,
Though silence lingers deep.

OLD TREES

THE BRUSH which paints the sky each day
Has also drawn the distant hills
Where many flowers bloom in May
And nature offers verdant thrills.

A playful child once sought the shade
Of elder oaks and poplar trees;
He's the same man who craves the glade
Once his mundane ambition flees.

He walked through life while chasing dreams
Which all belonged to other men.
Now that his time has passed, he seems
Inclined to be a child again.

He often walks in his old age
And stops for rest upon the bench
Where, once, his dreams were set to stage
And leafy shade his troubles quenched.

His hurried years have passed away
And those old trees are all that's left.
He weeps and wants another May
When a small child in their shade slept.

VISION IN THE FOREST

a parody of Henry Wadsworth Longfellow

ONE DAY, in the woods, I heard chatter, and seeing
Shrubs move on a trail, came across the famed dwelling
Of elves, those immortal, most bashful of beings
Defending the mountains and darkness dispelling.

Two fanciful creatures of myth were together,
With hair soft as sunlight and robes in rich fettle;
They played in the meadows, refreshed by the weather,
And butterflies came in their closeness to settle.

I sought to remain in my hiding, enchanted
By beauty and wisdom refused to the mortal.
Alas, I was seen and with scorn reprimanded,
Forbidden to enter their magical portal.

I left as I envied the luck which is granted
To some, here on earth, by the whim of blind forces,
While others must suffer the seed which is planted
In frail hearts to stir and enflame new remorses.

SLIGHTED ARTIST

a tribute to William Cowper

OBSCURED BY curtains in a squalid room,
Ignored and trampled on by those above,
The slighted artist has no place to bloom
And no confessor for his need of love.

He roams the streets at night in search of friends
Who might remind him of a brighter day.
At last he turns around, goes home, and spends
His time in flights of fancy far away.

At day his torpid mind is irked and bored
By ramblings born of dull and witless thoughts
And he'd prefer to be at once ignored
By men whose dreams by vanity are fraught.

THE PHILOSOPHER'S LAMENT

a scene from antiquity

AS THE sun fades over waters and birds chatter in the grove,
Two old, wrinkled, weary thinkers wander slowly by the cove.
Waves advancing and receding from the edges of the sea
Bring a bittersweet reminder of the things which failed to be.

Like the gloom of spreading tempests, they see history unfold,
Over men's destinies, passions, unforgiving scepter hold.
As a cloud of heavy darkness on the limitless expanse,
Present, past, the very future are but pebbles in their hands.

To a bench in the old harbor they descend and take a seat,
Where their troubles they unburden every time they chance to meet.
One aged master stands in wonder at the beauty of the view,
While the other starts, with sadness, his life's story to review:

"Hatred, envy, dread and fire, painful things I understand
And the soul's most secret workings I can write out in the sand.
But, despite this precious knowledge and insight, I have a fetter
Which, insulting, reprimanding, I must carry to the letter."

"For too long I've lived on Patmos isolated like a ghost
And by high decree commanded here to languish by the coast!
Once renowned and well respected, in academies received,
All I have now is the shadow of the glories I have lived."

"Bold discourses, fine attire, admiration from great men
Were all lost and I was given in exchange a prison den
And, from all the wondrous splendor and richesse of Roman art,
I was taken to the gallows by a soldier in a cart."

"Much as I had put my people and my honor above all,
Not a single word or action could at last prevent my fall,
For inside the Coliseum and the marble halls of Rome
A new cult and gravest danger, uninvited, found a home."

"Surging waves of superstition from the Great Sea's eastern banks
Have for many years infested all the army and its ranks.
Countless monks and shrewd fanatics with no passion for our culture
Have for three centuries labored to dethrone the Roman vulture."

"From Hibernia to Egypt, from Hispania all egregious,
Many fools and witless beggars have in stupor joined their aegis.
Marble statues of the heroes—the art treasures of the world—
Were by angry hammers tortured and their stone in markets sold."

"And the efforts of the Senate to extinguish all this fury
  Were frustrated by convictions that their god would promptly hurry
  To reward and praise the burning of the books in Caesar's hall:
  Pliny, Tacitus and Thallus, and to rescue from the Fall—"

"Man, who, to their minds, with weakness and with infamy is covered,
  And who cannot live in honor unless by this faith recovered.
  Who are they to claim such knowledge, to proclaim us in the dark,
  When their theory of Nature is that all came from an Ark?!"

"Odes to Bacchus might be pointless if the gods did not exist,
  But by what right do they reckon that we too are lost in mist?
  As to man, by what concoction fabricated in the East
  Do they claim the noblest creature to be little more than beast?"

"Where, in man, they see a squalid, unrequited, dismal creature,
  I see beauty and much noble to admire in every feature.
  They see tragedy and error, unrestraint, reasons for shame;
  I see Venus and Apollo, Hercules and nothing lame."

"They maintain that their religion by their Providence emerged,
  That by Christus their dominion on the Empire has resurged,
  While I know—as well as any who our history has seen—
  That by cunning, fraud and scheming all our power wrought has been."

"And when I, of all the people in the Senate, singly durst
  Ridicule their machinations and attack, and be the first
  To tell Caesar in plain language before all the Roman world
  That our handsome Roman eagle was as good as dead and cold—"

"If our homeland and our temples were prostrated before fools,
  I was met with shouts of anger and then banished from the schools
  Of great learning—where for decades I had been among the teachers—
  By a hoard of angry peasants, of archbishops and of preachers."

"With feigned meekness and forgiveness or with pity condescending,
  I was exiled here on Patmos, where perchance I might find mending
  For my sins through deep reflection and by holy intermission
  Of their saints: those sordid creatures who had lost their full cognition,"

"And, especially, above them, by that man with wicked lips
  Who in caves upon this island had composed th' Apocalypse.
  But no matter... It is written: 'One weak man against the age
  Is a galley in the tempest, a faint scribble on a page.' "

"Despite all I've done for country, for my people and for man,
  I was cursed to see the epoch when this great decay began
  And to know that, from now onwards, the great marvels Rome achieved
  Will in time fade into ruin and their mem'ry disbelieved."

"All I have left is the knowledge that I did what I was meant
 Without grandiose illusions that to Earth I had been sent
 By their Christus or by Mithras, as within a greater scheme
 At whose pinnacle their popery might imply that I had been—"

"If I had received their dogmas. Woe to those who, plotting thus,
 Now rejoice that they have triumphed over Jove and over us,
 For one day their own religion with derision, scorn will meet;
 Centuries from now, all mankind will be told of their deceit!"

"What they have achieved by sending an old man into exile
 Others will repeat by methods far more brutal and more vile.
 Helios will rise and set on generations, generations,
 And in due course all their stories will be snubbed by every nation."

"And when all civilization has shrugged off this superstition,
 Only then my life and grind will have accomplished their full mission.
 Then shall I, like the great heroes, rest in peace fully avenged,
 When all fear and guilt have faded and our dim fate has been changed."

With these words of grief and anger, the old man concludes his speech
While the sturdy waves of autumn splash their foam upon the beach.
After listening in silence, his companion then sighs
And, with sympathetic gestures, he turns forth and he replies:

68

"You have suffered long in silence on this wretched isle, my friend,
  Yet an olive branch for succor and reprieve I'd still extend!
  Men who would abuse religion shall abound in every age;
  When unrained by laws, they always treat the world as their own stage."

"Wicked minds of their conviction and of ours exist as well,
  And when they might hark to meekness not one soul can ever tell.
  Many faiths and creeds shall blossom in the centuries to come,
  But the battle against blindness of the mind cannot be won."

"Was their cruelty incited by the nature of their cult?
  I would say that their minds' dullness brought about this grim result.
  Our own gods and many others have and will be yet invoked
  And, in their names, many nations will be deemed forever yoked."

"As you say, on many kingdoms and proud lands the sun will reign,
  Yet, in all, deceptive rulers Heaven's leave and nod will claim.
  They will bind their every subject to their taxes and their laws:
  By perversion of religion they will spread their wicked claws."

"Your chagrin was not incited by their faith or by their Lord:
  Dipped in bigotry and falsehood is the sharp blade of their sword!
  Whole millennia may follow before rulers understand
  That, to gain our true acceptance, they should never raise their hand."

"Though the arts and the fine letters of great Rome may turn to dust,
　Is there truly any culture whose great deeds are bound to last?
　In both near and distant future, some will think that their own world
　Might survive for many æons without falling to the sword."

"What our history has proven, and shall demonstrate again,
　Is that even kings can vanish unrecorded by the pen.
　Vain, indeed, are men's desires and their fantasies on earth:
　Unto certain death and ruin we are destined from our birth!"

OLDEN AGE

SUCH FANTASY within a dream is life:
A journey through the clouded paths of time,
The unrequited call of foreign lands,
Which only the free spirit understands
When mind and body both are in their prime
And yearnings do not bear the scars of strife.

When reason, though, stirs up in olden age
And the first snowfall gathers on the ground,
When cranes and skittish geese desert their place,
The heavy haze is torn asunder to make space
For childish wishes, treasures to be found,
And younger actors full of vigor on the stage.

REVERIE

THE SUN has set behind the golden hills
And silence reigns within the forest deep;
The dice of life fall as the goddess wills.

The shadow grows, the birds are fast asleep:
A somber night is beckoned by the breeze;
It's direful from the cup of lore to seep.

The wind of autumn murmurs through the trees
Adorned by rusty leafage on their crowns;
Alone are those whom secret wisdom frees.

Upon the lake, dim whispers softly drown
In playful croaks of frogs around the shore;
Accursed is he on whom sly Venus frowns.

The goddess moves, her silence to restore
And soothe the vulgar crowd into repose;
Unwise it is her wishes to ignore.

THE TEMPLE OF THE MUSES

a tribute to George Gordon Byron

THE TEMPLE of the muses stands forsaken.
The souls which filled its vast and gilded halls
Are scattered thin or by time's sickle taken,
For few remain who answer to their calls.

These walls were built by men of ages past.
Their taste and sense of beauty were admired,
Their rhyme and talent truly unsurpassed;
From those today much more should be desired.

Unworthy figures who now hold the seats
Of those who gave the centuries their glory
Parade unhinged to spread their cheap deceits
While bookshelves fill with dull, plebeian stories.

FOE AND POSTERITY

BRIGHT IN the sky is the menacing moon,
Forced and relentless the winter night stride.
Rushing, the enemy's bound to be soon
   Close to the traveler's hide.

Wearied and breathless, he throws off his gear,
Besieged by the cold. He loads up his gun
While mumbling a prayer, but fate's drawing near:
   Hope for escape there is none.

No quarter or pity! His dear one is far,
His life nearly over, his eyes stern and bleak.
Death, foe and posterity merciless are,
   Yet none shall remember him weak.

PYRAMIDS

a tribute to Percy Bysshe Shelley

HOW VAIN and foolish is the man
Who craves and fancies that his deeds
Outlast him through the ages can,
Persistent as the pyramids.

For even what the pharaoh built
Is buried deep and lost today,
Effaced or maimed by time and silt
And victim surely to decay.

What little verse is left for thought
Will rarely bear the poet's name;
The long-forgotten script cannot
Propel the ancient bard to fame.

Yet many men can never change
What lies within their boastful hearts,
And those who live must taste the range
Of grim distaste, which pride imparts.

MOTHERHOOD

THOUGH WE were close, I left so long ago!
Our memories, once bright, now barely glow.
The smallest chance to meet again shall be
The gift of love which you still have for me.

From early childhood I grew up with you;
From you I learned all which is good and true.
Time's flow cannot efface our happy past,
Though our long lives forever cannot last.

Soon I shall be again in your embrace,
And my warm hands will comfort your dear face;
Yet always, in my heart, I shall regret
My old mistakes, though kindly, you forget.

LOST FRIENDSHIP

I THINK so often of our past,
Of how much time had drawn us near;
I would have never thought I'd hear
That our close friendship would not last.

The dreary autumn rain was falling
That fateful day, when we first met.
Who would have known your heart was set
To disobey my strongest calling?

We were each other's secret then;
To us, the world was dead and hollow.
And there was never any sorrow,
Nor any sign it would all end.

So many years have since elapsed!
You are now happy with another,
But I still won't forget, but rather
Recall the beauty of our past.

REQUIEM

A MAN once pondered
   His fate and scars
As his mind wandered,
   Drawn by the stars.

Gazing in sorrow
   Up at the moon,
He mourned the morrow
   Ever too soon.

Warmth and seclusion
   Were his to seek,
Golden illusions
   When days grew bleak.

Many reflections
   Swelled from his past:
Dire recollections,
   Forceful and vast.

Silence and stillness
   Haunt him again:
Such is his illness,
   His requiem.

MISGIVINGS

WORDS OFTEN used to chide a child
   Grew deep within his soul
Where—as their taste was never mild—
   They took a hefty toll.

They never meant or mattered much
   To those who caused him pain,
Yet, full of scorn, they swiftly touched
   And made him grieve in vain.

From those few words grew up in him
   Misgivings deep and great
Which filled his life's cup to the brim
   And made him weep with hate.

Throughout his youth and later days
   He tried to break the curse
Which cast him into its dark maze
   And claimed his universe.

Now old, he may perceive at last
    The irony of fate,
Though many tests he had to pass
    His heart to liberate.

What might seem harmless at first sight
    Can cause a heavy scar
Which throws the soul into the night
    And makes it stray afar.

Once time has passed, there's no return
    To childhood's fleeting days;
Let every soul amain discern
    The coarseness of its ways.

A FAIR AND BLAMELESS GIRL

a parody of William Wordsworth

SHE WAS a fair and blameless girl:
   An angel to adore
Who trumped in worth the rarest pearl
   Like no one else before.

Her parents lived, both old and frail,
   Though steadfast to the core,
And her heart ached to see them ail
   Like no one else before.

The mother drew her last, sad breath,
   Her soul ordained to soar;
The daughter lived and mourned her death
   Like no one else before.

Distraught and weak, the father died
   Still haunted by a war,
And the poor daughter wept and sighed
   Like no one else before.

Her cherished dreams were swept away
   And shattered on the floor;
Since then, she dreads the coming day
   Like no one else before.

Her story is but only one
   Among an ocean more,
And yet she saw her world undone
   Like no one else before.

RHYME

SOME warn that everything's been said,
    But others disagree.
Many would claim that rhyme is dead;
    I want to wait and see.

Some thoughts are harder to convey
    When prosody abides,
Yet should one choose to throw away
    The beauty it provides...?